Get Awesome

Get Awesome

Above and Beyond: Where Passions Meet Purpose

Jeff Lavin

Published by Game Changer Publishing

ISBN: 978-1-7365491-6-2

GC Game Changer
PUBLISHING
www.PublishABestSellingBook.com

DEDICATION

To my parents, family, and my friends, thank you for always encouraging me to pursue my dreams. For my friends that are no longer here, I'll continue to carry the sword in your honor. Butterfly, thanks for challenging me. Finally, to everyone reading this, here's to you, I dare you to dream just a little bit bigger and reach a little bit further.

DOWNLOAD YOUR FREE GIFTS

Read This First

Just to say thanks for buying and reading my book, I would like to give you a free bonus gift 100% FREE, no strings attached!

To Download Now, Visit:

www.Passionsmeetpurpose.com/freegift

Get Awesome

Above and Beyond: Where Passions Meet Purpose

Jeff Lavin

GC | Game Changer
PUBLISHING

www.PublishABestSellingBook.com

Foreword

I have had the pleasure of knowing Jeff personally & working with him on various projects that required an intense amount of energy, innovative thinking, and real-time results. He lives, breathes, and very much is giving you the modern playbook to winning Gold on any stage in life.

This isn't going to give you someone else's million steps to nowhere - this is a guidebook to use and reuse over and over again!

Get Awesome is THE on-time anthem for THIS MOMENT in HISTORY! Anyone who is ready to unapologetically and intentionally take mastery of self-positioning seriously and is unafraid to unapologetically rise to the occasion, this clarion call is for you!

Following through this is a fast forward guide to making the gap between passion and purpose disappear on purpose!

You picked up this book for a reason, and it matters! Get prepared to think, to rethink, to embrace this as your process towards getting awesome on purpose! The moment is now. You are your first step forward into a new horizon! Congratulations on taking initiative. #GetAwesome

Dr. Davia Coutcher, MPNLP MCBTP
International Bestselling Author
Unstoppable Gems
Wealthy Women Success Principles

Table of Contents

Introduction

Hey, what's up, everyone? Jeff Lavin, and I'm super excited that you're reading this book. These are the skills I've used in life, snowboarding, and in business. Once up a time in a galaxy far, far away, for one second, I was on the top of the snowboarding game by creating a move called the backside double cork. What I want to share with you by writing this book is that unstoppable mindset. I took this unstoppable mindset to go above and beyond, not just in athletics, but everything I do in life, everything I do in business. How we do anything is how we do everything.

I remember when I first got into exploring the mountaineering side of snowboarding. Sometimes we'd hike 4000 vertical feet to our descent point. It was uphill and tough, but everything worthwhile is uphill. I've been saying that a lot lately because it's a fact. Almost everything that has value, almost everything that has purpose, requires work on our part to obtain it. We have to put in the effort to get where we want to go.

Think about it. Do you want a good marriage? You have to work at it. Do you want a good career? You have to work at it. Do you want to change your life, achieve a goal, do something you've never done before? You have to work at it.

Nothing good in life comes easy. And very little that comes easy is good. Everything worthwhile is uphill, which means you have to choose to go and get it. It's a motion of left foot, right foot, one foot in front of the other, one step at a time. You have to grow and stretch yourself a little bit every day. You may not conquer that mountain at first, but with every hill you climb, you build that confidence for the next one. And then there's another to climb from the bottom up.

Yes, it's a fact anything worthwhile is hard, but with the right mindset, steps, and tools, we can accomplish almost anything. I thought long and hard about this process that I've used to overcome the most difficult obstacles since I can remember going back to childhood.

I've put together 11 steps that I took to go from 0 to 100 to the top. They will help you dig deep internally, build that solid mindset, create the map, those first steps all the way to the top. My goal is to help you eliminate the impossible and make it possible by empowering your inner I-M to make it possible. Are you ready to finally get out of your way and kick all those doors down? To go above and beyond? To climb up, go through it, around it, below it, whatever it takes to hit your goal.

Let's do this, let's go, let's get to work, and Get Awesome!

CHAPTER ONE

Living In The Moment

THE FIRST STEP FOR MANY IS investing in yourself. I both congratulate and commend you on embracing your personal development journey. The first step is *presence*. There's a saying, "Yesterday is history, tomorrow is a mystery, today is the present." Often we don't realize the significance of the moment until it's passed, only to look back and realize how rare that moment was. Have you ever had something pass you by in the blink of an eye? It's okay. It happened to me quite a bit too.

The present isn't always perfect. Wars are going on somewhere on the planet, children starving, masses of email messages piling up in your inbox, you can't stand your job, and your business is in a downward spiral. While we can't change the past, we can learn from it. The past is history, and we're meant to learn from it rather than repeat it.

We can look at the downside. Sure, the glass is half empty, but what if it was half full? The great part about the present is we can control and adjust it. It starts within. It's all about that attitude of gratitude. We can make an impact; feed starving children, master that job, build that business. You're so close, don't throw in the towel. That breakdown of the wall or barrier is upon you.

Here are a few skills you can work on to fill the glass: Practice, Patience, Persistence. These will keep you present. Think about it as you're living in the moment and just being there, being 100% there. There's no past, no future, just right now, in the purest of nanoseconds. How I would explain is what we call Flow. One of the things that I found out how to do just in athletics and then snowboarding was really slowing down time and really focusing on that. How I did that was practice. I practiced day in, day out, three times a day. I made sure I had those reps to where you could do it in your sleep, to where you could dream it, to where you could wake up and just go out there and get it. I knew it forwards, backwards, inside, outside, in between. It was all about creating that muscle memory and the visual cues of spotting where I needed to be in the air, on an element, or taking my line.

Okay, so how does this relate to you? Every chance you get, take those reps, read that script, rehearse it in your mind, and create that visualization. What's it feel like? What does it look like? Is there a color? Are there people with you when you hit your goal? Do they Cheer?

My first Backside 720 that I landed perfect, I got lucky, but I wasn't always lucky. I was the klutzy kid growing up. My father taught me patience early on. Patience was a big thing cause you're going to fall. You're going to fall short; you're going to get knocked down, but you got to know that eventually, you're going to get there, you're going to come through. As the saying goes, Rome wasn't built in a day, and that's okay. No one's a failure who gets back up. The biggest failure is not getting back up and giving up.

That's where persistence is so clutch. Persistence is just getting up time after time, after time, even when you're tired, powering through, coming out, and getting after it. Even on your bad days, even on your worst days, even on your off days, just making sure that you're getting in there, you're getting those reps, and you're getting that time there. Practice, patience, persistence for me is what it took. You will have that breakthrough moment where all of a sudden, all those stars align.

Belief. Belief is something that I built from practice, patience, and persistence. Do you believe in yourself? I often found myself questioning whether I could, should, or if it were possible. As long as I had the foundation of all of the three above, then I'd give myself the pep talk to believe. Believing in ourselves and others is such a powerful force. Think about it. That's why there's a flag on the moon, why we created and innovated as a society.

Belief is what it takes to overcome the other side of fear. On the other side is freedom. Freedom is where the fun happens. It doesn't have to be a 120-foot gap. It can be something like sharing a one-minute story with a group of people.

It was 2002. Here I was thinking about this, this wild and crazy move, something that would set me apart from the others. I had no idea how to do it, and I became obsessed, eventually dreaming about it. I built up to it with the steps above and made it happen a couple of years later, in 2005.

Everybody said this isn't possible, but I crossed that out of my mind. I said, "I'm going to make that possible. I'm going to go that extra in ordinary to become extraordinary. I'm going to land this!" Jumping was never really my forte. I was always doing rails or other stuff like that, but I said, "I'm gonna do this! I'm gonna get this!" It was a lot of visualization of just pure, pure, pure living in the moment and seeing this through. In snowboarding, especially jumping, there's this saying of "approach, takeoff, maneuver, landing." You can counter. You can relate that to life.

In business, I called it my business plan or prospecting plan. How do you approach them? The approach sets up everything for success. A bad approach on a jump, well, the rest isn't going to go well. Same with business, or anything in life. Think of it like approaching a new person, maybe to ask them out. You wouldn't ask them to marry you right off the bat.

Once you have a solid approach, it's time to take off. How do you put that action into springing off? It's the ask, it's action, putting it out there in the universe. Your approach sets up the success for the takeoff, a.k.a the action. From there, in snowboarding, we call it the maneuver. This is where the fun and the pure moment happens, spinning, flipping, flying, and so on. How does that relate to you? It's how you respond to what you put out there for the takeoff, a.k.a action. It's the debate, responding, handling objections, flowing, and being present. Time slows down, no matter what for me. This is often in business where my flow is negotiation.

How do you make that springboard and then your maneuver where that's the moment right there, because that's where everything happens. Time slows down. So what I really saw was nanoseconds to everybody's quick seconds. So you see it as, you know, a couple of seconds for me. I slow that down to about two minutes. Just being in that whole flow. Before I land, everything picks back up. So I learned how to do that a lot in life, whether I'm speaking on stage, or having that ability to kind of forecast with business deals or seeing what's ahead, it's just taking the anticipation and then knowing that you have that right there in that moment.

Now that we've covered the action items you can build on, let's talk about the attraction items that it builds. Manifesting attracts. People are attracted to happy, positive people, and positivity attracts positivity. What are you manifesting and saying to yourself? As the saying goes, thoughts become things. Anytime I drop in on my board, I say, "Think and feel the outcome." I don't do it until I feel it!

I've always found that what I put my energy into comes back in one way or another. For example, do you put your energy into positive things like helping others? It may not come back from the person in a reciprocal manner, but the universe has a way of sending it back when you need it. Everything works in a balanced cycle. We must appreciate and enjoy what we have now, and always with the goals we want to achieve down the road and in the future. It's great to think about them, to strive and work towards them. I try to avoid feeling anxious, desperate, or obsessed in a way that overwhelms my focus away from the now. Plain and simple, follow your heart and gut. That intuition has an amazing way of leading you to where you're meant to be. Overanalysis will lead to paralysis. I count to three, and if I feel it, I go for it.

With snowboarding, surfing, being outside, I always found myself in harmony with my environment. Riding big mountain backcountry lines, I view it as I'm working together with the mountain to create. Same with surfing, the ocean is a living, breathing organism, and I'm coexisting in harmony with it. By aligning myself with my source of energy, it brings that harmony. Everything is connected by energy. What's your environment that brings that to you? Find it, tap into it. It brings the best out in us. It will allow you to tap into your real power!

Eventually, I could only ride at a certain level or progress to a point where the high risk, the high reward was worth it. What I found was I still had influence and a following. With snowboarding, you can only do this for so long. There are only so many moments you can live in, and there are only so many glory days. Don't get me wrong, it was a fun highlight, an awesome time of my life, but eventually, a boy breaks down. So that's where I found myself getting into business, getting into marketing, getting into all sorts of other amazing stuff. I started my snowboard brand, where I was able to pass that forward and help other people create and help them find that within themselves through coaching, our athletes, and everything. And then we found that successful blueprint of how do we market this snowboard brand?

How do we share this? How do I build my personal brand as an athlete?

My next step was, how do I become a superstar marketer? That's where we came up with the Influencer Academy. It was actually created out of a challenge. I had a friend who said, "Hey, you're (expletive) brilliant! What's holding you back?"

There was a time in 2018, I had some rough patches and stuff like that and was kind of figuring that all out. But when she asked me that question, I just really sat there and contemplated it. And I said, "What *is* holding me back? What's stopping us from creating. What's stopping me from helping and from serving my purpose?" And that's where it hit me like a lightning bolt. I was standing on the stairs, I just got out of the gym, I was visiting friends out in Wisconsin, and I said, "Holy cow, all that stuff that we do or that I've known how to do, we gotta teach that. We gotta teach people how to be present in the present, how to live in that moment, how to slow down time, how to get that approach to that maneuver, that landing, and how to stick that!" Whether it's athletics, whether it's chasing that dream of starting your own business, whether it's closing that deal, or just in everyday life, we all want this.

All right. So let me tell you about where we took that presence and living in the moment. We took that and applied that to Influencer Academy. You can check it out at realinfluenceracademy.com. The sole intent and purpose of this was to help people find that unbreakable, unstoppable mindset, along with the "how-tos" of building systems and processes. To go above and beyond, but also to have the tools because anytime I looked for the tools out there within the marketing world, I couldn't find them, And if I did find them, they were outrageously expensive. So we decided to help create something to serve the masses, level the playing field, and make it accessible for everyone. Not only do you have personal development, but there's also some amazing automation in there, like one of our courses, *Automation Domination*, where we show how to build that brand. It shows you how to find that niche, how to find that avatar, how to really help push yourself.

Let's talk about the imposter mindset, that mindset of doubt. I wake up with that every day, but there's some stuff I do to get above and beyond that by living in the moment and being present. In the Influencer Academy, it came to be. An amazing person challenged me. She just said, "Hey, you're brilliant! What's stopping you? What's (expletive) stopping you from hitting the top?"

At the time, I kinda made a long-winded excuse. I made like the longest 20-minute excuse I ever came up with. My friend called me on it, saying I was just making up excuse after excuse after excuse. The truth is, if I'm doing this, then how many other people are doing the same thing? But what if we could all live at our optimized, one hundred percent full potential? We created this to help you be your best in that present moment. To help you get that practice, to help you build that patience, to keep you going with that persistence, to build that belief, and to chase those fears, whatever it is in your life— closing that $10 million deal—closing that $100 million deal— building that house of your dreams—creating that business or asking that amazing person to marry you, whatever it is, that's what this is for. Live for the moment, and create more amazing moments. Life's a paintbrush. Time is our canvas. We only go around once on this magic rock around the bright shiny star. Make it count, make an impact. Stop playing small, skipping that rock on the lake, and think about the tidal waves you can make when we live up to our full potential. You're amazing, full of greatness. You've got this!

CHAPTER TWO

The Evolution Sparks The Revolution

WHAT'S THE EVOLUTION that sparks the revolution? We all have that one breakthrough that connects the dots and opens up the doors. That moment when you finally get it. What really sparks that? We all have these crazy, crazy, crazy moments where life happens. Sometimes you just get that pure flow moment where the universe or whatever you want to believe in, just gives you that something. Maybe it's that move you're working on as a snowboarder, maybe that lead comes through, or something along those lines happens. The evolution sparked the revolution that I went through as an athlete, the ups and downs that treat your body like a rental car.

The high risk, high reward works when you land and walk away to play another day. Go big or go home, but sometimes you go home with crutches. You see us pull off that perfect maneuver, but you don't know that I went through back-to-back ACL surgeries to come back to compete.

I'm going to kind of segue really quick into Get Awesome/WI-ME, my brand that we created. I just really found that whole clarity and that whole purpose. And it's what really made me realize that life is fragile, and we only get so much time around that bright, shiny star on this crazy magic rock.

So in 2016, our team manager, Dustin (an amazing guy), we connected in Argentina many years prior. We just became really, really good friends. Like one of those people you just meet, and you hit it off, and you're inseparable like peas and carrots. Even though you didn't spend a lot of time together all the time, you pick up where you left off in every conversation. In 2016 Dustin was diagnosed with stage two colon cancer. Amazingly, he kicked! But he actually changed his whole lifestyle, his eating habits. I watched him get on Keto. He got into the best shape I'd ever seen him in doing a whole bunch of pull-ups, working out, just really figuring out what his whole foundation was body wise.

Fast forward a couple of years later, circumstances changed again. Cancer is one of those things. Some people are lucky enough to beat it, but unfortunately for Dustin, it came back. He had tumors on his liver and his abdominal wall. At the time, he had a one-year-old son. Now, when I was growing up, my dad traveled a lot for work. So, I thought, *holy cow*, I just want this kid to know his dad, and this dad know his kid, and we're gonna do everything we can with our brand to help him, to spread this word because we all have our fourth quarters, you know, those moments when your back is against the wall, and there's not much you can do but fight and come back. Sometimes you're lucky to make that comeback when that final clock strikes zero. Other times, you're not.

We did everything we could to help him fight that battle. We helped him with his treatments, raised money by donating boards, raffled boards, we even made the straps for the keir board. But it was one of those things where as soon as we launched that board, the next day, he passed. It breaks my heart that his son's never going to have his dad, and he's never going to see him grow up or any of that stuff. That's so, so tough.

One of the toughest things I chose to do was close out his celebration of life. I knew I had something to tie everything and every one of us together. Where to go from here? I got up, super nervous, I almost lost my thoughts, but it became clear. Dustin touched us all in one way or another. He was a thoughtful and selfless person who'd give you the shirt off his back. Some of us he helped more than once. I said it's incumbent upon us to continue to carry that sword, fight the good fight, and never forget this legacy by continuing it on as we all individually saw fit.

Think about what you've done, who you've impacted, the lives of others you've touched. There's a day that will come for all of us when it's all said and done. What will your legacy be? What will they say about you?

This got me thinking long and hard. I have causes, and the ability to make a difference, an impact. So that's where I found that my purpose was really helping people, and that's what I wanted to do with our brand.

Even though Dustin lost to cancer, he won by how he lived life with the values, virtues, and integrity he shared with us, and I do my best to carry that sword. We march into battle, and we fight in his honor, and we fight to create that legacy. And those people who are fighting it, we tell them, "Hey, you got this, we're with you. We'll fight with you. We'll cheer for you, man." It got me thinking. It got us thinking about other stuff too. I was speaking with a good colleague of mine who's a blogger. I said, "Hey, Jeff, you know, suicide rates in mountain towns are way higher. Especially for men, it's nine to one versus anywhere else." We were talking about why that would be, trying to figure out all that? I said, "Hey buddy, some people are going to see the things the way they are and ask, 'Why?' I'm going to dream things that never were and say, "Why not?"

It didn't end there. We made that another cause to fight for suicide awareness, especially in the mountain towns. We let people know, "Call us, talk to us. Here's the number, spread the word, create this community. Talk to these people, be there," because it's a paradise and can oftentimes be lonely.

And then from there, we have a lot of women writers and women fans, and they said, "We'd love to get involved with domestic violence. It's huge up here. It's big in these towns, and nobody's really talking about it. Can you help us?"

I said, "Absolutely. And while we're at it, I have a friend who's battling breast cancer. Let's support boarding for breast cancer." So we found these causes that were near and dear to us. And you really have to think, what are those causes in this? What's your why? What's your why for existing. So me helping people and connecting with people, that's my sole purpose. That's why I survived all the crap that I've been through from so many accidents, near-death experiences, all that. Why are you here? Why does the universe have you here? Why does God or the Creator, whatever you believe, why are you here? And this is something you have to do. You have to think long, deep, and hard where you take a number like 64, and eventually, you're going to get a one or ultimately a zero. You gotta get down to that whole foundation and think to yourself, what's that thing that really irks you? What makes you get out of bed? What's your why? What's your purpose? That's what this whole exercise is about. It's finding you, connecting with you, connecting deep inside, and saying, "What can I do? Why am I here? Where do I want to go?" Because I can tell you, once you have this, you're unstoppable. You're like a freight train. You're like a massive ship, an airplane. Nobody can get in your way. I mean, they can slow you down, but you're unstoppable. Once you have this at your core, it comes from the heart, and it comes from deep down inside. You have to find that, and you have to dig deep, deep, deep down inside and think, who am I? Why am I here?

CHAPTER THREE

You Better Believe It, You Can Achieve it

LIMITING BELIEFS FOR ME go back to childhood. Some of them were so repressed it took me forever to figure out what was stopping my success. It was the fear of success. That's the right, the fear of success. I feared success, not failure. What are your limiting beliefs? We've experienced those traumas, and some will even say traumas that are passed down generations. Here's mine.

I grew up in the Midwest in Janesville, Wisconsin. I wasn't athletic or scholastic whatsoever. I was quite behind my peers and a total klutz. The stuff my teachers and my peers said often got into my head. I'd cry alone after school or write "I'm stupid" in my notebook because that's what I heard. Can you imagine the self-esteem I had? It wasn't that awesome. Two things came really easy for me, snowsports and watersports. Growing up with them, maybe I was born for it, or starting at an early age might have helped. On the snow and water, I was free and could fly into my own adventures of my imagination.

I was also a product of my environment, a tough, blue-collar town with places such as the General Motors assembly plant, factory work, agriculture, it was tough, but it made me who I am today. I was picked on quite a bit in elementary school because I was smaller, slower, and a total klutz. At an early age, I found my freedom by not feeding into it. Growing up, like any of us did, I was a product of my environment, in a land of limiting beliefs. You get quite a bit of people pushing you to settle early on. It's how it was done in a lot of places. It still is, but holding people back from their dreams is unacceptable. We are all capable of greatness. I had a group of friends that would shoot down a lot of stuff that I thought about. Teachers, counselors, educators, even coaches would say, "No way." When I stopped listening to them and letting them get into my head, I started winning!

Eventually, you have to figure out what you're going to do. Since I was two or three, I loved electronics, played with flashlights, ripped stuff apart, figuring out how it worked from backward, forward, inside out. Dyslexia is classified as a disability. I say it's an ability and a gift. Same with ADHD, the ability to hyperfocus and live in the moment is amazing.

Do you have a crazy pipe dream? I sure did, being a snowboarder and making money doing it. Who told you it's a pipe dream? Because you shouldn't tell that to yourself. I grew up on snow with my family. I started skiing at two and a half. I always wanted to be on snow, hoping to be a pro skier. Eventually, in the 90s, I found snowboarding because of skating, and I was that awkward kid who couldn't talk to girls, that seventh grader, 13-year-old who said, "Hey, you know what?

If I can get really good at snowboarding, I can talk to girls." It didn't necessarily work out that way. I got really good at snowboarding and am still figuring out how to talk to women (haha). Such is life.

I always had the dream that I would be published in a magazine and be in movies. This is before the X Games, but I'm going to go do something on the snowboard. I want to do this. Kind of the way we announce those big goals to our friends or circle of friends and peers. A lot of them said, "What the heck, Jeff? How is this even possible, man? What are you thinkin' bro? You can't do that. We don't even have snow. How are you going to do that? How are you getting in these films? How are you going to get in these competitions? How are you going to train? When all we have is 500, 800 vertical feet. It's not a lot. I mean, these are garbage dumps with chairlifts on top of them."

It's not what you do with a mountain, it's what you have as your goal. It's inside of you. That's kind of when I learned early on that we are the sum of the people we surround ourselves with. It always gets me thinking about crab fishing, because well, you get one, you got to put the lid on it, but you get two, three, four, five, six, seven, a dozen guess what? You can leave that lid off. Because when any of them try to crawl out, another one pulls it down. We have to ask ourselves, who are those people dragging you down, and who are the ones bringing you up? And that's where I found a whole different transition. When I went to the East coast where it wasn't what you had, who you were, it was "Hey, what can you do?"

That was just a total stark contrast of going from the Midwest to I have this, and this is my status, I'm defined by my material stuff, to now I'm defined by what I can do. I found a lot of people there in my peer group pulling me up, and I never, ever, ever could have gone and crushed it the way I did. We also have to think about traumas and dramas. What's happened to you? I mean, what have you gone through?

When I was 14, I was on a boat. It was August 3rd, 1996, and I was with my friend and my family. I don't remember a heck of a lot of this, but from what I've been told, we were hit from behind on the Rock River, and I sustained one heck of a concussion to where I had no idea where the heck I was. Those braces that kinda made me that ashamed, quiet kid who didn't like to smile a lot, that perfect smile that I had? It went away. I had that overbite again and a whole lot of memory loss for about six months. I didn't remember who I was sometimes or where I was. I had an image that this must be what it's like to have Alzheimer's or dementia. You walk to your best friend's backyard, it was across the street from you, and you have no idea where the heck you are. So that's trauma. That's something I had to overcome. There is a fear of getting hurt. There's a lot of fear, you know, I placed behind myself where I said, "I don't know. I don't know if I can do this." I didn't waterski or go on boats for a long time after that. You know, going fast on those, I was afraid. Eventually, I had to face those fears. Eventually, there was stuff that I loved more than that. I'm one of those guys that is kind of a risk-taker who treated my body like a rental car.

So, fast forward, four years later to 2000, I'm out tubing behind a truck. The first couple of times worked out amazing. We thought we invented a whole new sport. Third time, totally different zone or a different location, rope connected with that tree. Perfect. The biggest tree there. And as luck would have it, boom! I got laid out pretty hard, and I had a punctured lung, lacerated liver, and ruptured renal artery in my right kidney. At the time, I didn't know the extent of the injuries. Being 18, I thought this is nothing. Like when you knock the wind out of yourself or with broken ribs, but my breath wasn't coming back. It was getting worse. My right lung was filling up with blood. It was getting hard to breathe.

Somehow I managed to walk into the hospital on my own accord. I was in pain like you would never believe. No matter what they gave me, every five minutes, the pain kept coming back and coming back for seven to 10 days or so. I was in and out of consciousness. I was in the ICU, and wow! That completely changed my life for a long time. I think it was harder on many people who saw it, that knew me, but I was in the hospital for a good month in pain. It was a constant thing to where I was prescribed morphine. And then the last year of high school, I was placed on regular Oxycontin where I'd get the hot sweats, cold sweats, all that just to relieve the pain. Eventually, it stopped the pain that I felt inside of my body and replaced it with the pain of addiction—the addiction to those narcotics that my body now needed.

Getting beyond that trauma took me another year or two because, in my twenties, I think I was 20 or 21, I still wanted to become a pro snowboarder. I had to get beyond that. I had to do a lot of work. I had to do a lot of practice, surrounding myself with the right people. I had to get away from those people who dragged me down, that told me I'd never amount to anything other than working in that auto plant or living in that town and having ten kids or whatever. That whatever suits anybody, but that wasn't for me. I knew there was more out there. There's more that I had to get out there. And I had to get beyond these limiting beliefs. I had to get beyond the limiting beliefs of what I was told and what I was programmed. We have to get beyond those limiting beliefs of what we're told at an early age that you can't, you can't, you can't, you can't.

But what if somebody told you, you can? What if they told you there's a chance? What if you told yourself you can? What if instead of looking at the glass as half empty, someone told you the glass half full? Who are you surrounding yourself with? Can they bring you up? Are they bringing you down? Who are your friends? Who are your mentors? Who are your coaches? We all need those five, those five people. That's what I learned early on. I needed some friends. I needed some cheerleaders. Well, first, I needed a mentor. I needed the person with that blueprint, the success, the time, the experience, and all that. And then everyone needs a coach, and the coach might have some of that same stuff a mentor did, but he or she can push your buttons. They can make you do stuff that you normally couldn't do. They got that direct connection to your head and then are cheerleaders on your worst day, on your best day. You know what? Sometimes we get our ass kicked like Rocky by Mr. T, but there's always Apollo Creed helping us get back up.

So sometimes you get your ass kicked. Sometimes you have a great day, but no matter what, those people are still there to cheer you on. And then there are your friends. There was that one speech where I was rhyming something or doing something funny or if you've ever heard me karaoke? "Well, you cleared the building again, Jeff." That's what my best friend Gary says. "Yep. He cleared the bar out," or "I'm a poet, didn't even know it." So finding those limiting beliefs, what are you saying to yourself? Who you surround yourself with? Are you saying yes? Are you saying no? Are you saying you can versus you can't? It's really just sometimes it's crossing off a letter. Sometimes impossible is just, I am. Sometimes to be extraordinary, I have to go a little bit extra. You got this, find those limiting beliefs. Find that stuff, use that why? And those limiting beliefs and watch, watch, watch what you can become, watch where you can go.

All right, awesome. Once you find those limiting beliefs, whether they're on the surface or they're very deep, I guarantee you the more work, the deeper you dig, the better results you're going to have from this. One of the things I always say to myself, and I'm going to say it to you, unsubscribe from those naysayers, subscribe to the yay-sayers. Listen to the people who tell you that you "will do," "you got this," versus the ones that sell that negative BS. You don't need them. You don't need them in your life.

Eventually, my favorite thing to do is to prove them wrong, to prove the haters wrong. There was a time when I had come back from ACL surgeries. If you don't know what that is, that's where your anterior cruciate ligament gets replaced in your knee. I lived my first one on February 24th, 2006. And then I got my second one, my left one, December 12th, 2006. There were people who questioned whether it'd be possible to make a comeback. Others said, "Oh, you're done. You're done. You're gone. When are you going to get a real job? When are you going to get a different hobby? When are you gonna become like one of us and give up on your goal or never get off the bench?"

And I said, "You know what? Never! I'm going to take this, and I'm going to go to the gym and think about every word. Anytime somebody said, 'Hey, when are you going to get a real job?' And I'm going to go do some real cardio. I'm going to do some real weightlifting. I thought about that in my head over and over and over when I was doing rehab or physical therapy, thinking about that, doing my exercises over and over and over "When are you going to get a real job? When are you going to get a real job? When are you gonna get a different hobby? When are you going to give up? When are you going to quit?" Never, never. I'm never going to quit. I'm always going to keep going and use that negative. I'd use that negativity and a form of what I call transmutation. I take that energy and all that bad stuff and use that to fuel my fire and turn that into pure, positive energy and love.

It might not be athletics. It might not be this, but I can tell you, one thing the world needs a heck of a lot more of is this. We have to take all this bad, all this wrong, and rechannel that, rather than focusing on it. Saying this person said that, or that person said this to us, no. Be the change you want to see. Everything I've overcome, I've been able to transmute that sad song and not just make it a good song, but make it the most number one, kick-ass, chart-topping, the best one out there.

What are the limiting beliefs you were told? The ones since childhood? Dig deep, the subliminal ones? If you have that mindset, find those beliefs, and then start thinking, *all right, what can I do to rebuild this foundation? What can I do? Who can I surround myself with?* Because I can tell you it's like jet fuel. And if you want to go to the moon, you're going to go to Pluto instead, once you learn how to use that and harness that.

CHAPTER FOUR

The Mindset Grindset

I ALWAYS SAY, AND IT'S NOT ME, I've heard it many places, that thoughts become things. What we think when we dream, what we say, will become reality. It all starts with this mind and the crazy mindset that's unbreakable. And for me, there's a huge, huge aspect that I play into that where one of the best things I can give you is gratitude. Gratitude. Just being thankful. Being thankful for everyday life that you can get out of bed, you can brush your teeth, drive a car, or shoot that basketball. You can walk, you can run, you can change that remote on that TV, you can drive to work. You have to think somewhere out there somebody isn't physically able or mentally able to, or both.

Where did I learn this? The big thing was a TBI concussion I had in '96 and that boat accident. I had a complete rewire and rethink of who I am? *Who is Jeff Lavin? And how do I learn? How do I do stuff?* Thank goodness I was 14, but holy cow, I wouldn't wish this on anybody to go through this. I had no long-term or short-term memory, what I learned or who I talked to the day before, I forgot the next day. I think there's a movie out there, like 51st dates or 31st dates, or one of those. It was literally like living that movie, but the doctors said I would get better, so you can move on from that.

For me, rewiring the brain was such a huge life hack where I said, all right, I'm going to do stuff, to memorize stuff. A friend of mine would play the memory game with me. He would ask me, "Hey, do you remember that time when we were five, and you did this, and you did that? Eventually, it got to the point where we could just name off months and years. "Remember that time in '93, it was June, and you did this, and you caught that fish," those crazy memories. But by continually remembering stuff, remembering the past is essential. I was remembering and visualizing and memorizing stuff. So the big thing for me was just learning how to be that crazy learner to where I could memorize stuff and see the words as they were spoken or stuff written on the board on the inside of the building. I could draw back and replay it out of my memory.

Eventually, that type of stuff, whether I was doing designs or working with equipment, helped me later in life. I could look at a piece of machinery and tell myself that once I knew how this works, I could completely go and redesign it, revamp it and redo it. For some people, I mean, if this is how you learn? That's cool. Take those notes. But there's a lot that happens from pen to paper. For me, just hearing that word, seeing that word as a spoken process, it's a full playback of what happened day by day, moment by moment. We all have ways to capture stuff, but some of the exercises that I do allow me to memorize that. For me, my past is a huge, huge part of who I am.

Think back to your earliest memories. I remember my first dream when I was one and a half, and I was in a totally different house and sitting in my high chair. And then I woke up in a different high chair, and I was like, "Whoa, what was that?" But that always is one that just kind of hits me. It's my very first memory. So, think about the first time you dreamed or the last time that you remembered your dream, the last time that you had that real good dream or that real good REM sleep. Think about that, remember that. All right.

Think about your earliest childhood memory. Was it good? Was it bad? Think about the one that made you happy. Think about the one that made you sad or made you mad. All those emotions we feel or think about. Think about the one that gave you gratitude. Our mind is powerful. If I can do this, if I can rewire my brain, so can you. It just takes a little bit of work doing one thing a day. Maybe it's crossword puzzles, or for me, it's exercise; the mind is an amazing thing. If you don't use it, well, I guess you lose it. I'm not a doctor, I can't say that, but that's just how it works for me. So we're always doing fun stuff, rhyming, minimal screen time, all sorts of fun exercises that just make us think. When's the last time you read? When's the last time you read or talked or sang? Sometimes you just have to put those creative juices to flow.

What are you thankful for? That's the big part about this. For me, I'm thankful for my mind. What are you thankful for? What makes you happy? Is this something simple? I love that I can brush my teeth. Sometimes that electric toothbrush runs out of juice, and I just move my mouth and my head back and forth; It makes me laugh. I'll scream, "Woo!" You would have thought I won the Super Bowl. Everybody in my household, or if I had visitors over, they're like, "What's going on with Jeff? He just got out of bed. What's going on in there?" I guess everybody's kind of used to it by now. They know I'm just excited to get up. I'm excited to move around. I'm excited for this new morning. Are you a morning person? Are you a night person? Are you an afternoon person? Where's your energy flow? Do you know your energy flow?

I wasn't always a morning person. I used to be the biggest afternoon and night person, but that kind of changes with age. Now, I'm a morning person. You should hear some of the music I play. Everything is those super, super happy songs. Those make me excited. What are you listening to? What are you doing? What are you doing to find that gratitude? What are you doing to psych yourself up? Because that's what it takes. It takes that excitement, happiness, and good vibes. I need to feel that good sensation to have that good experience, that good memory. If you conquer finding and overcoming your limiting beliefs, could that help? When you tie that together with your mindset, can that help? Once you've exposed all those and work on those, work on this gratitude. Do you tell people that you appreciate them? How many people do you tell, "Hey, I love you." I tell a lot of people that. I might not see him until tomorrow, and I'm like, "Hey, I love you, man."

They're like, "What are you not going to see him until next year or something?"

"No, I just say that all the time." When I get done after pounding a set, I'll say, "Hey, love you, man. I hope all is well, check you tomorrow." Right on. That's what it's all about, gratitude, loving yourself, loving others, and sharing that love in this world.

CHAPTER FIVE

Blazing Your Own Trail

OUR CORE DESIRES WILL lead us to amazing destinations. What does it take? What's it entail? What's it all about? For me, I'm a big, big believer in positive affirmations, saying the universe has me do this. If I'm good to others, basically the golden rule, which is, "Do unto others as you would have them do unto you." If you see somebody in need of a hand, give them a hand, help that neighbor. Help that elderly neighbor shovel their driveway. Help those around us, but also help ourselves. We often forget about ourselves. One must fill up their cup before they can fill the cups of others. What do you do to fill yours?

Some positive affirmations I say to myself, "I got this, I'm going to crush this. I'm going to do this. Let's do this, let's go!" Whatever it is, whatever it takes, what do you say to yourself to make you happy, to get you stoked, to make you amped, make you pumped, to make you want to go out there and to get it? What are those words? What do they look like? How do they make you feel? Do they make you excited, or do they make you want to tear it up?

Take ten things here, ten words. For me, I'm going to go with stoked, excited, pumped, amped, and rad. I'm going to throw in awesome. Those are mine. And then suck, bummer, drag, take those other words and cross those off. Think about the positive ones. Rad. Stoked. Amped. Think about that peer vibe, that pure essence, and tell yourself, "Yeah, I'm going to do this. I'm going to rock this. I'm going to crush this. I'm going to be awesome at this. I'm going to go so huge on this job, and it's going to be the best. I'm going to rock the crap out of this." That's what you have to say to yourself. "I got this." How many times do you say, "I got this?"

Have you ever done anything? Golf, boarding, jumping into a pool, anything like that? I can tell you the one thing that holds you back is not having that good word, that good vibe, that affirmation. But when you have that positive vibe, that positive affirmation of, "I'm gonna rock this, I'm gonna crush this. I'm going to do this. I'm going to knock this out of the park," you probably are. If you can't come up with those words, even with golf, sometimes just get up there and do it before you can say anything negative to yourself and then visualize. Visualizing was essential to me while I was on my board. I'd say, "All right, great. I have to do backs. Yeah. I have to do a 900," which is two and a half spans, taking out backward, landing backward. What if I just broke that down? That'd be a mathlete, not an athlete, but that would be five 180s, or that could be a 450 or a 360, that could be this and that. I could add those on together once I had the key understanding of breaking it down and then playing it back together. It was easy.

What are the steps that you're visualizing to get you to your goal? For me, I visualize my run where I'd have to take this jump, hit that rail, or sometimes to be on the big mounds where I had to avoid this rock. If you hit this rock, you're going to die. Or don't fall here, that's not a good spot, but over there, those are the amazing sweet spots. So it was a visualization of seeing myself and seeing others and seeing how it worked. Maybe you're not doing this entirely, but what is it that you want with your goal, with your desires? What's it look like? Maybe it's buying a house. What's the color of the paint on the walls? Is there a fence? Is there grass? Is it by the ocean? Is it in the mountains? Is it out in a beautiful pasture, thousands of acres, a whole lot of corn around? Maybe you want a farm. Maybe it's in business. What's that business look like? Is it ten people? Is it a hundred people? Are you the next fortune 500 company? Even Mr. Amazon had a visualization. This is an excellent way to get a great understanding of this. Think about it this way. We're all getting older. We're going to graduate high school or college. Well, that's four years. Okay. Break that down to the core. Break it out into semesters, break it down into quarters, break it down into mini quarters, break down two weeks, break down a day. What's that look like? What's that look like for what you want? Where do you want to be? When do you want to be there? And work backward.

For me, I'm going to become an awesome mega Uber pro-do-something guy when I'm 22 or 23. I knew what I had to do to get there, working forward to backward. It's like going into an NFL game or a baseball game or a soccer game or anything out there. We always have a halftime where you can make quick little adjustments. The first quarter went awesome, or maybe the second quarter didn't go so awesome. What does it take to adjust that to make the next part rock? What's it take to do that? As an athlete, that was always, always, always huge. It also goes into fault versus responsibility. Let me share a story with you. And this is one that very few people know about. I was the victim of abuse at 21.

I was in a small town. I had a police officer who was a little touchy, feely in areas he shouldn't be. I can't explain what ran through my head then and there, it was either I'm going to harm this person seriously, maybe kill him, or I'm going to take off and run. So I ran, but I didn't talk for four days because I felt this guilt. This whole thing around me, like I wasn't in my own skin. But was I going to become a victim of it and allow it to consume me? It did for a little bit, but eventually, I forgive him. I don't want him to starve or die or anything like that. I just don't want him to eat at the same table as me. And there's a lot of us that have been wronged by people in our past or maybe bad circumstances, right? It's not your fault. That happens. It's not your fault that your dad was an alcoholic. It's not your fault your parents got divorced, but it is your responsibility to do something with it. It's your responsibility to take that and harness that and make that into the positive end of visualizing. What we can do to get the life we want and not let that get in our way. What are those positive words, those affirmations, those things that make you feel good? Are you visualizing? Do you have a plan to go from forward to backward? No plan works out crystal clear and perfect. And if you do find somebody that has that, let me know at Jefflavin.net. Email me because I want to meet that person.

We're always adjusting. We're always adjusting our plans. We're always adjusting from forward to backward to meet in between. Nothing has to work out perfectly to get you there. It's not the destination. It's the path we take. And what are you doing? Whose fault is it versus responsibility? What are you doing with that? Are you going to let it consume you? Do you want it to drag you down? Are you going to do something with it? You're going to turn it into something amazing.

CHAPTER SIX

Pep In Your Step

I USED TO SAY *RIDE, eat, sleep* in my heavy-hitting days on the hill. I'd ride to feed my movement, eat well to fuel up, and get plenty of sleep. It's that simple. Do you have a consistent regiment, or is it constantly changing? One of the hardest things I did one summer was a swing shift job, I could never get on a schedule, and my energy was diminished as a result.

Sleep health plays such a big part in what I need to perform at a high level. I can function well with 6 to 7 hours of sleep, but I need at least eight for the quick reactions. Same with speaking, thought leadership, or creating, sleep is a big part of my life. Getting those proper REM cycles, sometimes I find myself solving problems in my dreams.

Early on, I found how much huge value nutrition played in my life. We're all genomically composted differently. What works for you won't work for the other person. We all must find what works for each and every one of us! Combine that with drinking water, how much should you drink? Are you drinking enough?

When I think of good vibes, I like to think about the good vibe tribe, who are the people that I hang out with. The people who bring me up, the people who lift me up. What is your regiment? What are you doing to fill your cup, particularly the mind, the body, and soul? For me personal development, and continuously learning feeds my mind. Exercise and movement feed my body along with a good nutritional regiment and sleep schedule. Music, socializing, people, and laughing feeds my soul.

The times it takes, how long does it take? And do you have a positive attitude about that? Where do you love? What do you love? Where do you go? What do you do? How do you take that and make it yours? The good vibes. What are you asking yourself every day? All the affirmations, everything that we talked about above, what is that?

For me, I got to go back and talk about getting my butt kicked, knee surgeries, no fun.

I think that was six months on the first one, five, four and a half on the second one. It was less time on the second surgery because I knew all the stuff I could get away with and how much harder I could train and do on the second one after going through the first one. I remember the first one, just going through that, here I was on 4/20 of all days, knee's cut apart, and I'm like, "What the heck did I do to myself? I can't walk. I'm like Frankenstein. Will it get better or will it not?" I never was a guy that liked to sit on the couch. I'm always the guy that moves around, bikes, goes out and runs around, doesn't sit still. I had to slow down, but I gave it that much more when I was able to get back in the flow.

It was the same thing with the other knee. I was bummed that I couldn't go out there and prove them all wrong in 2006 and 2007, that I'd have to wait for another six, seven months just to show them what's up. But I never let those good vibes get away. I was always listening to that cheesy music. You know, those songs that make you laugh. There's always something out there that makes you laugh. There are people that make you smile. There's something that brings out that innerness of you. What is it? What are your good vibes all about? Who are you? What's all this good about you? What are those jokes? Where are those jokes that make the whole room laugh? What about that? That goofy dance. Maybe it's that goofy dance? There's something out there that makes you laugh, and laughter for me is so key for all this. The good vibes, the smiling, gratitude, happiness, thankfulness, bliss, dig deep.

Who are you? Create your most optimized you. Even when you've been down when you've got your butt kicked, what is it that makes you get back up and just laugh? Maybe it was playing soccer, and you got knocked down, or somebody slide tackled you, and you just laughed. Maybe you were skateboarding and fell, and you just laughed. Heck, I fall snowboarding, surfing, all that stuff, and I just laugh because it's funny. And I know I'm going to go back out there. I'm going to get it. So no matter what you have in front of you, adversity, what is it that makes you keep going?

Every one of us will have that moment that we're going to experience in our lives, and it's not going to be on a Friday or a Saturday. It's what you are going to do at eight o'clock on a Tuesday.

You got that call, but it wasn't a call that you wanted to get? What are you going to do? Maybe it's an internal thing. Maybe it's something external. Maybe it's something within your core, within your circle. What are you going to do every time? I always think, "Hey, I've had my moments. I've had these knee surgeries. I was backed up against the wall, 28 to 3, the third quarter is over, start of the fourth. You know what? The way I looked at it, I had 12 minutes left to prove them wrong. Twelve minutes to keep on going. Twelve minutes was 12 months. But at the end of that, that score is 29-28 because I had those good vibes. I had the time, and I had the grit to keep on going. So what're your good vibes? What's going to make you unstoppable when your back's up against the wall? Are you going to play your best game? Are you going to pull that trick out? Are you going to flip things around and completely do a 180 with your business? Maybe it's a relationship. Maybe it's a marriage. Maybe it's whatever you want in your life right now. What does it take to keep on going? What's it take to make that adjustment? Can you do it? That's where it all starts for me; good vibes and sharing good vibes. Because I know I'm going to give it my all, and sometimes it doesn't work out. Games, your love life, business, but you know what? I know I'm going to go out there, give my all, get my ass off that bench and do all I can to be the best athlete, the best significant other or spouse, to be the best businessman to make that deal, to help as many people as I can. The worst thing you can do is take no action. Get off that bench, and share you. So, are you going to do it?

CHAPTER SEVEN

Go With The Flow

GO WITH THE FLOW. We can only control the controllable. The universe has a way of flowing and leading us to where we're meant to be. Always trust your gut, and follow your heart. All too often, our heads get in the way.

What's your, why? That's a big point of this. You have to think, where do you find it? What keeps you going? Is it your family? Is it a significant other? What keeps you going? What gets you out of bed in the morning? For me, I dug deep a while ago, constantly looking to evolve, change, dig deeper into my why. It could change five, six, ten years from now. It could change tomorrow. It's all about finding that inspiration. What's getting you out of bed? What's making you excited?

So, where do I find my inspiration? My inspirations come from other people out there. I love listening to old speeches from authors like Hemingway or Mark Twain. Speeches from former presidents like Abraham Lincoln, JFK, and other leaders, Martin Luther King or Robert Kennedy. They all had amazing messages of unity. There's a lot of great thought leaders out there. Find them, find that influence, find those people that you kind of want to follow after and do what they did. It's kind of a copy and paste world we live in. Look how they talked, how they walked. It's not a fake thing until you make it that type of thing, but look at what they're doing. Look at what their success is. Study them, know them.

I always find inspiration in the simple little things when I'm out there. Have you ever walked by and saw a penny on the ground? Do you pick it up, or do you just say, "Nah, it's not worth my time." I'm going to get out my calculator here because I'm an athlete, not a mathlete. If you think about it, if you take a penny's worth, .01, multiplied by 60 seconds, that's 0.6. then multiply that, and then keep multiplying that, boom! You eventually start to see how that adds up that if you picked up every penny every day, it would add up to a much larger amount. Suddenly that small number is a large number, and it changes how you look at picking up that one single penny. That's the universe's way of telling you that good things are coming. When I see that change on the floor, I pick it up. The first thing I do is say, "Thank you, universe." Because Holy cow, the universe has gifted me with this money, with this abundance.

I've been into numerology. So I'm always looking at numbers, especially two, two, two, four, four, four, or 11 and 22. I look those up, and I say, "Oh yeah, this is awesome. This means I gotta keep on going on this path." And I've been seeing that lately, the universe, all around us, it gives us signs. So look for those signs, look for those signs and find that inspiration. Find that ever-growing, unstoppable thing that makes you like that freight train. Dig deep and think about it.

There's a lot of great mentorship. You can find it on YouTube videos, watch some of those, or you can read, there's a lot of great stuff out there. When I can, I'll take a look at my favorite people who influence me. I'm always being inspired by them and by other people. Then take that and pass it on to your circle. I'm always inspired by my mentors and people who have had success, the people who've made a hundred million dollars in real estate or people that have knocked it out of the park for personal development. But that's me, find what works for you. Maybe it's someone close to you, or maybe it's someone well known. I always strive for those who've had success before me as role models and examples. Then from there, I look for coaches. A coach will inspire the heck out of me because they know how to talk to me. And they know how to ask the right questions, say the right words, and push me to get those results.

Do you have a coach? That's what we're doing with Influencer Academy. We're putting together a cohesive coaching program to help you ask those questions, help you get those desired results, help you hit that development, and hit that next level in your life. And you know, it's a community, so you can meet some really cool friends and chat back and forth. And there's also some Facebook groups and stuff. Everybody needs the cheerleaders around them. So that's what we're building. We're aiming to build this goal of this Influencer Academy. We're aiming to build this as a community to help you develop, a community to help you hit that next level and an opportunity for you to remove that roadblock, to knock down that door. They say opportunity only knocks once, but opportunity should be a verb. You can make it happen any time. And you know who does the knocking? You do. And sometimes it's not knocking. Sometimes it's kicking down that door. Sometimes it's going over it. Sometimes it's going below it. Sometimes it's just building a whole new level of that house or that foundation and going for it. So that's our big goal. We're going to help you get aligned. We're going to help you get inspired daily, and we're going to help you build that influence.

CHAPTER EIGHT

Action, Cures Fears

MY WHOLE LIFE, I've always said, I'm just going to get off this damn bench and go for it. And success and failure come from the same thing, trying. There is no such thing as a failure if you're trying and you're getting out there. The biggest mistake or the most significant thing you can ever do is never take that action. Never do it. In our society, there's a big emphasis on failure. But is it really a failure if you flunked a test, you didn't get your driver's permit, or your business failed?

I'm going to look at that from the other side, from the other point, the other side of the coin. You can let that defeat define you, but I choose to let that complete me. Build off that because you tried, you know what not to do this next time, you know what to do differently, you know how to change that up. And as humans, when you were a kid, you didn't walk perfectly the first time. You don't run perfectly the first time. Maybe you rode a bike perfect for the first time, but let's be real, it doesn't happen like that. So we learned by failing and failing forward. Success and failure come from the same thing, trying. It's just looking at the other side of the coin, always looking at that action for me and curious fears. So I'm always out there and just going for it. So maybe I don't feel like going to the gym or going for that run or going for that bike ride or exercise or showing up on and off day. But I know if I do, that action will make me feel a whole hell of a lot better when I'm doing that activity. I'm doing it. I'm taking that chance.

Maybe there's a girl out there you like, but you're too afraid to put it out there. Maybe it's a business venture, some idea that you've had still stewing around for the past ten years. Maybe it's something that came to you instantaneously, but you're afraid to take that action because you're scared of that failure. Go for it, get off that bench, run with it. Part of success and failure and taking that action is also making the adjustments and making the adjustments as we go. I mean, have a game plan, obviously, but nothing ever goes according to plan. So have you planned? One thing I can think of in business was going back two years ago. I had a split with two of my former partners. One of the red flags out there that really stuck out in my mind towards the end was that we were out shopping for fruits and food to do barbecue or cookout. We purchased everything and went up to the self-checkout lane. I noticed someone had left $40. And me personally, whether it's a dollar, whether it's $5, whether it's a quarter, I would take that, and I'd bring that to the person that was in charge, just because I don't want that bad karma riding on me, not to mention it's theft. I don't want that negativity hanging on me. My former partner took it instantly and put it in his pocket.

A few seconds later, a lady approximately my mother's age came back in, and she was frantic. Who knows, that could have been her last $40 for the week. Meanwhile, my former partner was trying to play it off. He acted as if he never took it, and he had no idea what she was talking about. That's when I intervened. I said, "No, you're going to go give that back to her. We're going to have some big problems if you don't. I don't care how big of a fool you make yourself look like you're going to do that because that's what's right, that could be your mom. That could be your grandma. That's not right." So when you see red flags, those little things, it is a big red flag. For me, it was one that came way too late because if he were going to take that small amount from a total stranger, what would he do to somebody who he knows? Somebody in his circle of trust? What would he do? That left me feeling uneasy for the rest of the day, the rest of the week, the rest of the month.

As I started looking into our files and our finances, I started noticing inconsistencies. I started noticing problems. I started seeing a pattern, and around that same time, we had a disagreement on social media that just went on and on and on from his side. One of those deals and it was a complete and total embarrassment. Then somebody had notified me from one of our suppliers, "Hey, are you aware that (he) just sent us an email notifying us that you're going out of business and (he) is starting a new company? (He) contacted me to let me know that he started his own brand to let me know that your other partners are coming with him. They also want to use your technology, your innovations, your inventions, your intellectual property." Life can prepare us for difficult times, but it's how you respond to that email or message you get. I did some digging, deeper and deeper, and the house of cards fell hard.

Looking back, those red flags were there, a lot more than just the $40. There were some red flags here, red flags there, stuff that I kind of ignored or brushed off. And one of the big things, I had a gut feeling and something in my heart told me that it was off. So when you're out there taking that action, make sure you always follow your gut and your heart and look for those red flags you got in your heart. They never lead you wrong there. We have these for a reason, and they somehow know how to lead us where we're supposed to go.

While this was a negative experience, the outcome was positive. Sometimes we have things or people that hold us back. Make a note of it, and do what you can to remove bad habits and bad people from your life. Once you do, things become much more clear, and it paves the way for abundance. Once I was able to remove them from my life, I gained control of my company back and was able to steer it out of the storm and into better waters when I was back in the captain's seat.

Another thing that's key with action is what we do with our time. We all get the same amount of time in a second, minute, hour, day, week, and so on. It's what we do with it to maximize it to the full potential—setting out blocks of productivity for work, income-producing activities, time for physical activity. I'm a big proponent of using my calendars and schedulers for time management. There are some great scheduling apps that sync with electronic calendars. Then I have blocks where those are my time to focus flow while adding my daily time for surf, gym, etc. I keep all these blocks as nonnegotiables.

Distractions, shiny objects can bring action to a standstill. Think about creating an action plan, a blueprint similar to the way a house is built. There's the foundation, the things that are your foundation. Then the first story, this could be things you enjoy hobby-wise, family activity, etc. Then the second story, relaxation, things that fill your cup back up.

Recently I started using the 5 x 5 system for what I'm building with my business interests, and I'm incorporating it into my action plan. 5 x 5 comes from network marketing and building depth, but I found it relevant to planning. One week I focus on coaching, another week I focus on building our courses, then next, building my other streams of revenue, with one week to recoup and enjoy life while refilling my cup. We called it the 5 x 4!

Look for the flags, and signs, trust your gut, clear the clutter (people, habits), gain that clarity to take that action, and build that blueprint to maximize your action plan.

CHAPTER NINE

Send It

I HAD THIS AWESOME saying in my athletic career, and I try not to curse or say swear words a lot, but what the heck? It's something so simple that people would ask, "What are you gonna do? Are you gonna get up? Are you gonna go ride? What are you going to do when you can't get that backside 900? Or how do you keep on getting up and going and going? How do you have that courage and confidence?" Going back to like 2003, 2004, when I first turned pro in snowboarding, I would say, "Tuck it, huck it, fuck it!" That's pretty much the gist of it. This is my life mantra. I go in as fast as I can, you gotta tuck, you gotta tuck for speed and huck. That means ball up into the tightest, compact little ball that you can get into, grab both sides of the board and do whatever it takes, and fuck it! It might not work, but keep repeating steps one through two until you can, until you land it.

So that's my mantra for life, and it can be applied in business. Anything that you build, go as hard as you can, as fast as you can, and fuck it. It might not work out, but it's okay. That's part of failing forward. That's part of learning because you're just going to get better every time. There's a lot of stuff that we do, like self-sabotage. This was always something that helped that whole self-sabotage voice which says, "Oh, I can't do that, or I need to lose five pounds so I can do this new 10-80, or I have to build this much muscle, or I'm not perfect, or I'm not doing this move to the perfection of where I want to do it." Still, you just have to keep on doing one, two, three, tuck it, huck it, fuck it. Nothing feels better than just doing it. And just that pure action of living in the moment.

There's a lot of stuff we say to ourselves. There's a lot of stuff I used to say to myself, but you always have to look on the positive side of that. Are you saying, "I'm awesome"? Or are you saying, "I suck"? Are you saying, "I'm going to do this, I'm going to be the best at this." What were you saying before? "I'm going to do this. I got this. I'm going to run for this. I'm going to charge for it. I'm going to charge hard." Some men see things the way they are and ask, "Why?" I dream things that never were and say, "Why not?"

Think about the time when you were so excited that you did something. What was your posture like? How were you standing? Tall? Excited? Then think about a time where something didn't work out. What did that look like? How did you feel? Were you hunched over? Posture can change quite a bit of how we express our energy. A simple refresh of when it worked out and even a smile can change the entire vibe you express to others. Think about it, do you want to do business with someone who's excited, high vibe, and positive energy? Or the alternative, the person that's utterly defeated. Remember, even in failure, you've made it further having attempted because now you know what it takes. Take a deep breath and remap the game plan.

Few teams out there have undefeated seasons. When they lose, they readjust and recalibrate. Sometimes as humans, we must do the same.

I never believed in breathing and breathwork until I thought about it as an athlete. In addition, sports psychologists always mentioned how much it helped to take a few deep breaths before a run. Even the Apple watch has set times for breathing and being conscious of it. I find taking a second throughout the day helps quite a bit. If you want to explore breathwork further, there's a lot of great meditative tutorials and videos.

What can we do? What can we create? It's having that courage. It's what you're saying to yourself. It's having that confidence that's part of it too. It's having people around you who boost you up that helps. For me, there were a lot of videos where I'd videotape myself and watch myself do it over and over and over and over again until I got it the way I wanted. Eventually, I felt that confidence in my snowboarding career where I could ride and ride in front of people. There would be times when I knew it was off if I did something, but when I was on, I could really feel that. And I could feel that energy from everybody around me.

Later on, I took this whole out of body or the whole third-person perspective where I could view myself. I used that in business and in speaking. Sometimes I just filmed myself for countless hours if I had something to say. These days, we all got these crazy smartphones and devices in front of us. Everybody's got a video studio. Everybody has access to that. Use that phone, use that magical iPhone, Android, whatever it is, use that camera, film yourself, get that feedback, share it with your inner circle, your mentor, your coach. Maybe they can coach you on a few things and say, "Hey, that's cool. But I think this would be great if you adjusted A and B, where maybe if you did this a little bit different or executed this, then your end result could be that much more amazing." It's like getting the cherry on top of the hot fudge sundae with cream and then sharing that with your friends because they're going to tell you, "Bro, that sucked, but I love you. I'll buy a beer, but you'll nail it next time."

And then the cheerleaders, those are the people that even on your worst day, they're going to tell you, "You got this." Self-sabotage is real. It's a real thing. Just remember what you're saying to yourself. Just go for it. Nothing feels better than that action and going for it and chasing down that goal, chasing down your dream.

CHAPTER TEN

Trading In Excess For Success

YOU ARE RESPONSIBLE. You absorb your beliefs. You are in charge. You can accomplish incredible things. You can clear your thoughts. You can do the impossible. Whatever you imagine, you will manifest!

Accountability is a significant part of my life, and it's a major part of my success. So think about where you want to be. This is what I've always done. I always think about where I want to be. So think about where you want to be. Maybe it's a four-year goal or a five-year goal, right? And then break it down into multiple steps. For example, graduating from school, usually, that's a four-year endeavor. So you have semesters, quarters, stuff like that, and then break it down and work backward from that. That's a big part of my life and a big part of my success.

The other part is accountability. Do you have a partner? Do you have an accountability partner? I like to have somebody to hold me accountable for what I speak out there. Whether that's my mentors, my coaches, and definitely my friends. The cheerleaders are going to love me, whether I come up short or not. But I love having those people around me who say, "Hey, are you there yet? Are you there yet? Are you there yet? What's holding you up? What's holding you up? What's holding you up?" Part of how Influencer Academy came to be was one of my friends. She just said, "What are you doing? What's stopping you? What's slowing you down? What's keeping you from being your 100% best self, reaching your full potential?"

I thought about that, and I said, "Wow, wow, awesome. I'm going to have to get back. I'm going to have to get back to you on that."

So one of the things I love doing is saying the goals out loud to the world. Today it's easier because we have stuff like Facebook, Instagram, Twitter, and a whole social media where you can shout something out, and there are many people out there who pay attention because they follow you. Somebody might hold you accountable, but the best way to do that for me is I like to have my coach. One of the things we specialize in with Influencer Academy is holding you accountable for your goals. So, you can not only say it out loud to the world, but you can

also say it out loud to us. We can work with you. We can help you get there, whether it's hitting that million-dollar sales mark in your business or passing that $10 million goal. Maybe you just want to take it to that next level as an athlete, or maybe it's that relationship. Maybe it's working on that internal stuff. One of the cool things that I always did was align myself with good mentors. I surround myself with good coaches. I always had my parents, my family. They were always a big part of my accountability. I remember telling my grandma, "I'm going to do this pro snowboard thing. I'm going to chase a pipe dream. I'm going to do it. I'm going to do this. I got this." She never really understood it, just being from the Midwest and that whole way. She never really skied or snowboarded or spent time on the hill, so she didn't understand it.

But towards the end of her life, I remember I was talking with one of her friends, and we're talking about a mountain she knew, Saddleback, this place in Maine, and she knew snowboarding and knew what I was trying to do. At that point, I think my grandma realized this isn't just some hobby. This is kind of like baseball or football. She never got to see me reach that pinnacle or hit that top spot, hit that goal because she died the next day.

I held myself to that, and I said, "I'm going to do this. I'm going to do this." That made me push so freaking hard, so hard that all season 2003 to 2004, the level of progression that I hit, I used that to fuel me. I said, "Man, I'm going to do this. I'm going to do this." That was always in the back of my head that I'm doing this for grandma.

She passed at sunset, and coincidentally enough, my first published shot in Norway was that sunset. And at that point, I just knew the universe was aligning. It was behind me. I was hitting my goals. I was on track. I was on my way, and there is no better feeling than that. So I think about this. Do you have an accountability partner? Maybe it's a spouse. Maybe it's a good friend. I know for me, I have some of my good friends and colleagues who are my accountability partners. I also have a significant other. She's my accountability partner, big time. We have goals in business and other stuff and goals in our relationship. So there's that.

But also, do you have an accountability coach? I love having an accountability coach. Even at this level, you're always being coached. You're always being mentored. You're always being taught. That is why we're opening up Influencer Academy. We want to help you hit that next level in your life. Whatever that goal is, it's attainable. We're going to break down and rebuild that whole mindset, and we're going to help you crush that goal and knock it out of the park, and hit that next level of success. The key is to use this as a launchpad to push past life events and to build a solid future.

CHAPTER ELEVEN

Influence

RELATIONSHIPS ARE THE KEY to everything. There are four stages of awakening: Victimhood, Empowerment, Surrender, and Awakening.

As we build our mindset, as we build ourselves, we build ourselves to be unstoppable. This is one of the things I've learned just with the true connection. We've lost a lot of that connectivity through social media, through Instagram, Facebook, Twitter, all the apps out there, texting where that true connection is gone. It's still there, but it's not as prevalent as it once was, especially with everything that's going on with the pandemic.

As COVID-19 hit many of us, we've been relegated to our computers and our social media. One of the things that I've always taken with me and that's always helped me connect with people is rather than being interesting, be interested. Nobody loves a know-it-all. I mean, it's great if you know a lot of stuff, like the most interesting man in the world in the Dos Equis commercials, but rather than being interesting, be interested. Be interested in what other people do, be interested in them, and remember stuff. This is always something that has helped me when I talk with people. If you tell me, "Oh, my wife had surgery." I could see you a year or two years from now, and I'll ask, "Hey Lonnie, how's your wife doing?" People are kind of blown away that you've taken an interest in them by remembering names and stuff like that. That goes a long way and is better than saying sir ma'am, dude, bud, or bro. You're actually addressing people by their name and how they like to be called. So be interested instead of interesting and let that flow. It's all about making that genuine connection.

What about relationships with money? Do you have a good relationship with money? Are you saying, "Oh, poor me, poor me, poor me." I've been through that before. Two years ago, I played the victim for probably longer than I should have with my last business and splitting with my business partners. What are you saying to yourself? If you're in that constant victim mode or victimhood, it's going to be so tough to get out of that. You got to get the heck away from that and start thinking and saying, "This is what I have. I have a life. I can walk, I can brush my teeth. I can get out of bed. I'm healthy." You have to start looking at the other side of the coin.

The other thing I had to do was leave that ego at the door. We're building a business, building a brand. For me, I used to define myself by what I could do on my snowboard. If I can do that rodeo 720, then that was what defined me. But later on in life, I learned to check that ego at the door. And the big thing with relationships, what we can learn with ego is, are you going to act in anger? If somebody responds to you, are you going to take the higher road, or will you be the bigger person? In the past 15 years, I've done my best to practice unconditional love. That's a love you have for a pet, for a son, for a daughter, for a family member, or a significant other.

I was in a long relationship. We had both come from the same hometown. We both met out in the mountains but went to opposite high schools. I always felt that maybe that was destiny. Eventually, it came to the point where she wanted to live someplace else, and I wanted to live in a different place. I was out there catching the most amazing backcountry line. And I said, "Holy cow, that's freedom. This is awesome. This is amazing. She deserves that too." So I told myself to love her, I have to let her be free. And if we reconnect, great. That didn't happen. But we have a really great friendship, and I even spent time mountain biking and playing hockey and doing all sorts of other activities with her new significant other.

So, by leaving that ego at the door and checking it, my friend circle just grew. Are you practicing that unconditional love? Do you say no matter what, I wish you the best? If you get in an argument, you're never going to win getting in a fight or debating or any of that. Sometimes the best thing you can do is just listen or just take the high road. It's okay to lose with dignity and save that face. It's all right.

So the way forward, what we're going to do, we're going to take everything that we've been talking about, we're going to teach you how to knock this out of the park. We're going to find that presence. We're going to show you how to live in the moment. We're going to help you find that evolution that sparks a revolution inside of you.

We're going to find and help you overcome your limiting beliefs. We're going to build that mindset, that amazing, unstoppable mindset, and train you to get the life you desire. We'll teach you to find those good vibes, alignment, and inspiration. Learn to build up that courage, and confidence where you're no longer the cowardly lion. You're going to run towards the other side of fear because on the other side of fear is freedom and building up that accountability and mastery and knocking it out.

So that's what we do here at the Influencer Academy. We're here to help you take it to that next level, to be unstoppable, be unbreakable. To do this time after time, over and over again with this methodology.

Conclusion

THANK YOU SO MUCH for reading this book. You probably feel massively overwhelmed, and there's a lot of this to absorb and take in. Awesome. It's all right. I've been there. We've all been there. So the next steps, I'm going to lay this out, but first, I'm going to put a little bit of perspective on this so you can choose to take action or choose not to take action. Time's going to move forward whether or not you continue, whether or not you go with this or whether or not you take action.

Let's put this in perspective. Talk to the student that repeated a grade about the value of a year. Talk to the cancer patient about the value of a month. Talk to the weekly news editor about the value of a week. Talk to two people wanting to meet on their first date, about the value of an hour. Talk to somebody who missed their plane or train about the value of a minute. Talk to that person who got second place in the Olympics about the value of a nanosecond.

Yesterday is history, and tomorrow is a mystery. Today's a gift because it is the present. So to be the best present in the present, follow this link RealInfluencerAcademy.com. Follow the link to the

Influencer Academy. Book a call. Talk with one of our specialists. There's a free 45-minute clarity call that we want to give you as a gift for reading this book. So are you going to take action or not? Do you want that life? Do you want that goal? Let's do this. To all those cares that have been our concern, the work goes on, the cause endures, the hope still lives, and the dreams will never die. Let's make your dreams come true.

THANK YOU FOR READING MY BOOK!

DOWNLOAD YOUR FREE GIFTS

Read This First

Just to say thanks for buying and reading my book, I would like to give you a 100% bonus gift for FREE, no strings attached!

To Download Now, Visit:

www.Passionsmeetpurpose.com/freegift

I appreciate your interest in my book, and I value your feedback as it helps me improve future versions of this book. I would appreciate it if you could leave your invaluable review on Amazon.com with your feedback. Thank you!

www.ingramcontent.com/pod-product-compliance
Lightning Source LLC
Chambersburg PA
CBHW021140020426
42331CB00005B/844